WADING INTO THE LIGHT

ALSO BY MEL MCEVOY

An Emptied Space (Mudfog, 2012)

Wading Into the Light

Poems

Mel McEvoy

RED SQUIRREL PRESS

First published in 2022 by Red Squirrel Press
36 Elphinstone Crescent
Biggar
South Lanarkshire
ML12 6GU
www.redsquirrelpress.com

Layout, design and typesetting by Gerry Cambridge
gerry.cambridge@btinternet.com

Edited by Pauline Plummer

A CIP catalogue record for this book is available from
the British Library.

ISBN: 978 1 913632 182

Red Squirrel Press is committed to a sustainable future.
This publication is printed in the UK by Imprint Digital using
Forest Stewardship Council certificated paper.
www.digital.imprint.co.uk

CONTENTS

For those health professionals who dedicate their lives to looking after dying patients and their families

DIGGING UP MY GRANDMOTHER'S PAST

I

I bring dahlias for you
a handful of colour, smiling
scrape the moss hiding your name
speak to you softly with my fingers.

The bleached lichens
try to cover your letters
the only record on the landscape
that you ever existed.

I want to straighten
the hunchback lean
of your gravestone
still showing deference.

Your name glowed like turf on an open fire
when I mentioned our ancestry.
Old neighbours drew in closer,
poked your story in case they missed something.

My mother thought, you were her big sister.
She waited a lifetime, to be brought home
by someone who wanted her.
My wrapped arms could never find her.

She always felt the sudden ice
of nervousness, whenever she overheard
the slapped words: 'bastard' 'illegitimate'
point its finger, in mean conversations.

II

You cycled in from the country
hair laughing in the breeze
excited to leave your tight thatched origins,
proud to work 'in service' determined to impress.

Little Red Riding Hood set out innocently,
able to make exquisite cakes
in the politician's house, owner of the local paper,
whose son, the wolf, was dressed in grandma's clothes—

a bull in the field, humping
with no concern, whoever was available
especially the vulnerable,
without big brothers at home.

Taking the hats and coats
from priests and the town's powerful,
you kept your eyes low
from the scythe of the harsh stare.

The nuns worked you even harder
in their laundries for dirty linen,
gave barren couples your other children
but hid his name, in the folds of their silences.

III

Assembling half remembered rumour,
I find one line, in pride of place:
a family's well-kept sepulchre.
His chiselled name sneers at my approach:

'What are you doing here?
Who the fuck are you looking for?
What do you know about any of it?
Ya big gobshite.'

'Grandfather, I bring you presents:
a shovel in my right hand
a sledgehammer in my left,
but before I begin

I'll take a piss.'

A CHILD WITH A BALLOON

My mother
always kept
a tight hold on things.

Always listening
for any slight jab
of criticism.

I never once heard
the softness
of 'love' spoken.

Fifty years of watching
for her clenched hand
to open.

THE SHAPE AND SIZE OF MY SISTER'S COFFIN

Against the wall, near the door
a wooden radiogram appeared unexpectedly.

Under its lid, a swivelled radio dial searched
the outside world for words, songs, to fill   the void.

We waited
for the LP record
to slump onto the deck.

We entered its silence
between the gentle descent of the needle
and that first kiss of contact fuzz

and Johnny Cash's 'Ring of Fire'
galloped out, the length of the living room.

Whenever her name was mentioned
the arm was abruptly lifted   mid song.

NOBODY ASKED CAN THE CHILDREN HEAR

on the stairs
or listening in bedroom dark.

We dared not
                              descend
into tongues on fire
that would have devoured
any slight sight of us,

their rage rising
thumping the floorboards
swelling the wood
splintering into hearts
that couldn't hide quick enough
with hands over ears
under a heavy bus conductor's coat.

Returning to these roots
with my own children
I'm keeping guard
over their playing
at the top of the stairs
under the beds
near the grate
looking for my old heavy friend.

Why were there so many arguments
when we were children?

A vapour of petrol.

The heart runs looking for the coat.
Sentences spit and sizzle.
Floorboards mock this attempt

to try and tiptoe
down the stairs and ask:

how did my sister's dress catch fire?

HUMOUR RIDES HIS BLOOD

i.m. my father

in moments of conversations,
from innocent incidents
caught plucked and stored,

being pumped from the heart,
in an endless cycle
of stories: Irish
and entertaining.

In a chair he sits quietly
then unexpectedly shakes,
at times breathless,

the spirit
moving where it pleases.

Words made flesh
from the sudden flush
of another story.

MAM DID YOU FIND

a silence that loved you?

In the gathering around your bed
I could hear my heart
chasing after you
in the pauses between breaths.

When your absence
swallowed us up
I felt you entered deeper
into the-somewhere-else-in-us.

In the kitchen, unnoticed,
I listen for years
to your aggressive conversations,
long monologues, in voices not your own—

an inmate of your own asylum
trying to wriggle free
from the straitjacket of illegitimacy
in Ireland's finger-pointing thirties.

The last sounds:
a loud rattle of the hospital window
met a heavy rash of hailstones
and you were gone

looking for answers

and I bet

the angels fled.

I'M NOW PRAYING YOU WON'T HEAR HIM

Mrs Harman always stood on her doorstep, shielding the entrance, when in conversation with my mother. Her dark curtain-drawn house never had wide open arms but she always had enough sweets to fill the pockets of my short trousers. Always first in church on Sundays, drawn to the warmth of the candle rack at the feet of the Virgin Mary standing hard on the head of the snake. Her prayer, urgent, secretive: conversations among women. Bathed by the glow and hypnotic stare of the statue until her panic prayers slowed and caught up with her breathing.

Forty years on, in the last stages of cancer, she's still generous recalling to my mother what she caught me doing, as we sat beside her in front of her fire, visiting. Walking home from this last wave and door close, I heard about the prayers of those years.

Hail Mary, I am the sinner, the guilty one, the not good enough, ugly, fat one. It is all my fault. You have to punish me. I could have told the priest. I should have told the police even if he did kill me.

Hail Mary, he wants it all the time as if he'll die if he doesn't get it. He doesn't care if I'm sore or it's not the right time. I can't stop him. I'm too uncomfortable to sit for long on these pews. I can't stand his groping hands. Can't stand to get undressed in the same room. I think there is something wrong with him.

Hail Mary, my daughter's eyes feel like the tight squeeze angina makes in my chest. They look out from a cliff ledge and she won't take my hand. Something in her has died; there's an emptiness in her arms when we embrace. She says she can't stop listening out for his footsteps on the stair, even a hundred miles away, behind the tall stone walls of a Convent.

Hail Mary, being here makes me feel clean. I wash the priest's vestments as best I can. I love the rub of good cotton. He looks good on the altar in my work. I love to iron the small hand cloths with the little red cross. I like the sound the cruets make on the tray. I sometimes feel the candle wax is really weeping for me.

Hail Mary, a neighbour called today and I didn't mean to say as much as I did. She caught me with the chain down and not secure across the door. It was when her hand just touched mine gently that everything rushed out towards her. I couldn't stop telling. It was like talking to you. She just opened my windows, took my net curtains down to wash and the whole room was filled with light.

Hail Mary, there are no more secrets to tell. I can still hear the ghost of muffled sounds from my daughter's room. The cancer has savaged him quiet at last. He is in a lot of pain, sometimes I forget where I have put his tablets. Forgive me, I just can't pray he'll have a peaceful death.

SHE SEES WITH HER HEART

—For Helen from the monkey

Buy any toy you want in the whole shop.

In Woolworths every Saturday
the pink elephant would be so keen
to see her coming through the doors.
And always asked
if she was any better at French Skipping
and who was her best friend this week.

She loved that elephant
and knew where on the bed it would play.
She could put the whole of her hand
deep into its ears.

At the till, the daughter handed up
to her mother an ugly monkey
with hands and face of crude plastic.

I know I really, really, wanted Pinky
but who going to ever buy this monkey?
He's here every week, alone on the shelf.
No one will ever love it.
It's just so sad, I can't bear it.
He asked me to take him home.

Go get Pinky.
You've even made up a song about her.
You don't have to bring the monkey home.

Mum, he's asked me to marry him
after six weeks.

He's funny,
he never asks about my friends
or what I am good at.
His only suggestions
are about the wedding reception:
a bowl of nuts on each table
and for desert Banoffee pie.

THE FELLOWSHIP OF MEMORY

—For Paul my son

You never know
when the magic gathers
for moments he will unearth
from the riverbed of memory.

Together, on the horse
of his child-size bed,
ear and cheek
safe against my chest

chased by Orcs into darkness.

Still reading out loud
long after questions
and the light in caves
of heavy eyes dim,

pulling up covers
over shoulders
a closed hand buried deep
keeps safe the ring
with a wizard watching
from the outside of sleep.

YOUR GAZE KISSED THE LIGHT UNEXPECTEDLY

Your earrings
of aquamarine topaz and amber
speak to light
differently.

When my rogue words
leeched the liveliness
from your face
                                        you withdrew.

You emerge
back into being
where the light
surprises

as in the photo
on our bedroom wall
your older sisters in shadow.
You're about four
on your father's knee
held tight
shining.

I bring home
earrings of moonstone
and we try to find for one another
the glaze of petrol blue

playing
hide and seek.
with us.

DO YOUR OWN DEAD COME FOR YOU?

In a busy four-bedded hospital room
behind a single drawn curtain, she wanted
to talk with someone. Sent away the physio.

'Do you know what? I've had enough.
I'm sick of being breathless, tablets for every problem.
This heart struggles to get started on a morning.'

Vulnerability danced with honesty
and agreed there was only one road left.

'I'm not stupid. I realise I'm dying.
I'm still going to plant my tulips among his ashes.
Keeps the bugger busy until I meet him again.'

She was the teacher
and all of us in uniforms were her pupils.

'I must leave a tidy house, with all my bills paid.
Not looking forward to dying with an audience.
Can't stand all the fuss, like getting undressed in public.'

You sensed in an earthquake
she'd be the first to look for others.

'Come closer, you've still a few questions to answer:
without a body, how will we recognise each other?
Or does love know its way home in the dark?'

In the hush on the other side of the single curtain
the silence was filled with tulips.

LIVING IN AN EMPTY HOUSE

Occasionally, we'd catch a glimpse
of our mother at a window, waving.
Her life hadn't been lived in for years.
Every visit, we'd sit and try to reach her—
our words searched empty rooms.

She lived in a deep labyrinth.
There was always somewhere her feet were trying to get to.
She'd look up and smile at something familiar,
but then couldn't remember, losing names like her purse.
We all soon became lost.

A nurse saw the subtle shift, phoned in the early morning,
her breathing had quickened, her veins less prominent.
My sisters arrived on the next flight, afraid they might
have missed the bedside vigil. We tried to keep tight
hold of all the things she was.

We were coming indoors to our own expectations.
When without warning, she looked up
walked through our sadness, spoke to each of us
and relaxed in the final gathering. We ran
to her arms open wide.

She found her way home without directions
travelling light from the garden of forgetting
and stood briefly at her window, pleased with what she'd grown.

Waving

in the rest of our lives.

THE STORM

In a hospital side room,
on a continuous gust of oxygen:
Pulmonary Fibrosis was slowly closing your airways.

Struggled between breaths
to complete sentences
fear threatened to suffocate you.

Sweat seeped from your forehead
then you remembered feeling
like this, once before.

When I was in the Navy,
on a frigate in a force 10,
a cable snapped at the bow.

I was the only one trained to replace it.
Arctic ice drifted slowly past the vessel.
Couldn't keep my teeth still,
spanner and pliers were hard to handle.
Wave after wave wanted to drag me in.

Made a lunge for the cabin door.
Back inside, breathless, trembling
cold numb hands gripped the helm tight.

Being back on board
eased your breathing a little.
You whispered: *I'm not afraid of dying.*

I was so close before,
these blue tinged hands
are missing a steel cable.

Sit me more upright with pillows.
I need the table's edge to anchor me.
Let me see the horizon out the window.

HE SWIMS IN THE SILENCE

You sat in a wheelchair looking down from a hospital window at people walking seven floors below. A view from a diving board. You seemed too distant to turn when I introduced myself to your family.

I came to discuss a place in the hospice. Lung cancer had found a way to squeeze your spine from the inside.

Visitors spoke of your service to others. Nurses recalled how you taught them to swim as children in the local baths.

Generations knew your patience and for fun you swam the lakes of Cumbria.

Your wife said she felt you needed to talk. Thought you were drowning out in an ocean somewhere, adrift from everywhere. When the door closed behind her I sat and asked how you were doing. You looked out on the garden: we never spoke a word for twenty minutes. No splash of noise disturbed the hush. When she returned you spoke first and said: we have had a long chat and I feel ready.

A whisper of mist upon the lake and you waded out into the unthinkable.

ESCAPING UNNOTICED

You sat on a hospital bed, disorientated,
puzzling where to put your belongings,
nervous, anonymous, hidden within
the colourless clothes of the war years.

Uncertain, you watched where I placed
each item in your bedside locker.
You answered 'Yes' to everything.
Your sentences, lost in the fog of a stroke.

When your speech slowly returned
an accent came out of the shadows.

I asked would you mind if a male nurse
took you to the shower?

One arm reached across your breasts
so your hand could cover
the tattooed numbers on the other.

You led me to stand silently
beside you in the goods train
as you named all the companions around us.
There was a jolt and the door yanked open.

You were dragged from the box car
to march in line with others through iron gates
in the time it took, to shower, dry your hair
and guide your weak arm inside a clean nightdress.

Any sense of feeling safe was always beyond you.
You tried to anticipate the unexpected
and feared cold reasoning more than emotions.
Any uniformed soldier set off palpitations.

During the quiet early morning tour of sleeping patients,
checking for signs of pain or distress,
bed covers moved to rhythmical breathing but
from your room the silence dissolved into absence.

Although expected, you had escaped into the night
while no one was looking. I took your hand
still warm, knowing you were finally beyond
the dogs barking, the fence and the camp lights.

INFINITIVE

—The basic form of a verb, without an inflection binding it to a particular subject or tense

You're saying: I need the chemo.
If I don't take it, I'm likely to be dead by Christmas?

You're saying to have the abortion
or the drugs will kill the foetus?

We're saying: it's our only way
to have a real Christmas. Afterwards, we'll take our chances.

The hospice said it's ok to have her in the bed beside me.
Look! Her whole hand around my little finger is trying to keep me here.

I don't want to say this: I am not sure he loves her.
He looks so detached and angry. I hope he never comes to blames her.

i'm just saying they think i'm gone
but there is no here...and only the now

you can't be dead
when all the verbs are infinitives

DEAD MAN HAUNTED

He walks the hospice corridors all night, putting on lights, opening cupboards, checking no one's hiding. He hears pleading he wants to stifle.

Dozes during the day in the chair with one eye open. Looks as if he should have died a week ago. A frisson of something won't allow him peace. Family visit dutifully discuss nothing beyond the polite. His look makes the silence uncomfortable. Stepdaughter sits alone outside the room, disturbed as a snapped necklace, picking at scars on wrists.

Conversation in a jacuzzi while washing his hair:
'Your stepdaughter seems to be struggling. Would you like me to talk to her?"

'I know what you are up to. Get me fucking out of here. Now! Don't you go fucking talking to that lying bitch.'

I WISH YOU HADN'T TOLD ME

I hung up your fine clothes from Milan, shoes crowding the wardrobe floor. Givenchy stood on the toes of Gucci and Prada, restless to be out securing properties on Mayfair. On your head, a clump of thin dry grass, last year's nest.

I phoned the most expensive shops for an array of their most attractive wigs. Asked if someone could visit the hospice and fashion a hairstyle from a photo of you before the chemo. You enjoyed the stylist, being professional, giving you options, commenting on your Mickey Mouse slippers.

Told friends you felt safe. At times forgot you were bald. Your smile remained vigilant, even when your visitors had gone. Eyes closed in a bath, you said:

Promise me, when the time comes and I ask: am I dying? You will tell me the truth.

Among your family, you controlled the directions of conversation. Any future scenarios, you buried in long silences.

I was warned your condition had changed rapidly. Opened the door against the weight of hesitancy. Saw you leaning forward on a bedside table, waiting, breathless on maximum oxygen. Your eyes spoke of the promise.

I prayed the silence had hands to catch you. I nodded and let go of the rope with a slow 'Yes.' I thought you'd reached your own understanding and taken a hold on hope.

Thirty years tries to hide its one long moment. I can still see your eyes as they empty but it's me you took a hold of and won't let go.

IN THE MEN'S CLOTHING TENT

—Lesbos, December 2015

He doesn't want my help to step from the rubber dingy, waits for others and walks into the camp, cold, soaked with a bag of belongings.

It is difficult to understand the Arabic until he mimes avoiding the flight of Isis bullets in Mosul, ducking out of sight, making a run for it with a grandson in each hand.

Lifting up carefully a damp shirt over his head. Hasn't eaten much for months. His eighty-year-old skin, tough as dried-out shoe leather, with a visible railing of ribs. His vigilant eye is still without trust. He places his fingers over a swelling where a gun butt rammed the back of his head and describes how he kept hold of their hands.

I felt a desire to surprise such tenacity with the best garment left in the tent, the last set of thermal underwear, finest cotton, never been worn and around the neck a beautiful weave of silk still wrapped in tissue paper—fit for a sheikh.

There is laughter in the half dark. He approaches the other side of the counter. In a tense silence, arms raised with hands hidden in drooped sleeves, he protests. He is wearing an XL woman's thermals with scope for a large bust.

There is a quick search for something that fits. I seek forgiveness in an embrace, heads against each other. He has no desire to pull away but relaxes and through a smile comes a slow deep

'Shukran.'

Sonnets From a Hospital Lift

This single multi-part poem consists of a series of monologues in sonnet form that take place in a hospital lift. It aims to capture one episode of end-of-life care in an NHS hospital. The whole poem is an attempt to listen to the composite voice of a hospital. This collection brings together the voice of the lift and every person who enters into the lift. Together the voices portray the tale of a dying man visited by his wife, but it is equally about the lives of the professionals who care for this couple. The lift is a sentient being. The poem is a reflection on dying.

In this collection, there are fifteen poems composed of between two to three sonnets. The term sonnet is used loosely, but within each poem, every fourteen lines represents a sonnet even if it is a combination of two voices. There are forty-four sonnets throughout the sequence. The white page represents the shape of a physical lift. On the left margin is the voice of the lift and on the right in italics is the internal dialogue of those who enter. Each poem stands alone in its own right. Together they capture a series of interconnected events.

The poems represent a narrative of how people die in hospital and the care they receive. Each professional could have between five to ten of these narratives going on in any one week. There were 200,000 deaths in hospitals in England (2018) pre-pandemic. This is a reflection on a common experience.

SONNETS FROM A HOSPITAL LIFT

I

The lift is a confessional where feelings find words

Come, enter the emptiness,
find within the silence confidence
to let your feelings surface. The noise?
Only my stainless-steel doors closing.

Your fingers squeeze your locket together,
keeping the photo of you both, safe,
holding each other for better, for worse.

Hope you are going to be better today.
The house keeps asking questions:
the wind's rattling the letterbox,
wants to know where you are.
The moan of the radiator pipes is spiteful
saying: you're never coming home.
The jingling of the fridge makes me nervous.

The dog keeps sniffing the hospital bag.
Every morning your side of the bed
looks bereft, unruffled.
Even the flowers on the duvet look forlorn.

Breathe in deeply. Did you feel it?
That's me, raising you up.
Here, I am your thought-catcher
like a cathedral who gathers prayer.

For the first time in my dreams, we are not together.
I'm walking alone towards the end of a long pier
or waiting for your bus, but you never get off.

When you hung out his washing this morning
you forgot to lock the backdoor.

You've left the Lourdes water on the dresser.

II

A nurse from the Philippines plays the game of cricket at work

Come in, John Paul Rodriguez
eyes down on your phone for the cricket scores.
It's ten years, since we flew out to recruit you
from a country, dependent on remittance.

Still thinking of staying or just saving?
Your kids are laughing in the school playground.
You have a home on a nearby council estate
in one of the poorest areas in England.

You must have noticed, in the NHS
we try do things a little differently.
It's expected to be personal with strangers,
to find who's underneath the organs and illness.

So, when he bowls at you 'Am I getting worse?'
Resist the temptation, to duck the question.

He asked me: what was the point of all this exercise.
He just wanted to talk about the cricket.
He was sick of taking tablets.
I explained the importance of making an effort.
He felt too weak to walk the corridor.
I said: don't you want to live for as long as possible?

We talked about his innings.
I asked him how much had he told his wife but he gave me the umpire's finger.
I asked if he had any children but he just looked through me.

I could hear a wheeze and there was blood on his tissues.
I said I would put him in a shower
but he said he couldn't be bothered.

When I finished, he seemed to sense
he wasn't going to be long at the crease.

Your finger pressing my third-floor button
is the same number, John Paul, as your front door
back in the Philippines
six thousand seven hundred air miles away,
behind which your own elderly father waits
every night, to speak to you on Skype.
He's warned your mother, not to mention
what the doctor said about a triple bypass
and how much it was going to cost.

When you feel you've been thrown
a particularly derogatory comment,
you smile, lifting the bat high, to let it go wide,
knowing half of what you earn goes home
to put your younger brother through high school.

III

From the deepest places giving tries to fill an emptiness

Susan, Susan, of all the professionals
who look in my metal mirrors,
I sense you can see through
to somewhere different,
to where there is meaning
in the coincidence of chance situations.

In here, in this small confessional,
I hear the secrets and decisions
individuals cannot keep to themselves.

Sitting at the bedside of dying patients,
you are often given an open invitation
to enter into their diminishing world
and hear their choices and decisions
that have made them who they are.

He kept in place a high wall of bravado,
keeping those he loved on the other side.
He pretended nothing was serious
until I asked what his worst fear was:
not being forgiven for the things he'd done
and his wife on her own, finding him slumped in the chair.

The walls between us disappeared and he found himself
deep in the 'Soon' of 'Soon I won't be here.'

Dante accompanied Virgil
on his soul-searching journey
down through the many rings
of experience, to heal what was wounded,
and refashion an alternative ending
from one that seemed pre-determined.

Your compass is to listen, intimately,
and avoid the enticement of tangents,
walking silently beside anyone
into the fires of their deepest fears.

You are intuitive with every phrase,
tone, the length of every silence,
until the listener is convinced
that someone has found where they've been hiding.

Delicate conversations are like defusing a high explosive—
one wrong word and you are gone.

You look down into a chasm
of restless emptiness.
Your brother left when you were eight.
You were told to watch over him.
He ran out in front of a moment that had no future
for him and without any ending for you.
Now, you wander the landscapes of loss in others.

You stood on the banks of the River Styx
and have tried to bribe the ferry man
for a quick trip over or for any news.
He said, stay close to the dying
in moments when their speech seems confused
when they talk of relatives in a crowd waiting,
there, you might catch a glimpse of him, waving.

When we eased our way through the circles of his numbed silences,
he remembered his voice, belligerent and out of control.

I am an archaeologist for any small treasure of good acts,
sustenance, for this journey inward.

IV

The tops of bedside lockers sing about the unloved

Come on in, Helen, our secret chef.
A hospital is a hidden restaurant:
visiting wards instead of tables,
encouraging reluctant patients
to try the jazzed-up protein drinks,
to shake awake the elusive appetite.

You can immediately tell
how much a patient's loved:
an abundant bedside locker
means he's an oasis in someone's life.
An empty table with only water
is as barren as a mile of desert.

Here you're reluctant to leave, opening a hamper
of suggestions, wrapped in a generous smile.

If he doesn't eat, he won't get diarrhoea
and his wife won't have to wash his pyjamas.
If he pretends he's eaten, there's relief on her face
and he spends the rest of the visit,
trying to keep it there.

You explain the ingredients for life
minute material meandering down arteries:
calories, proteins, fats and carbohydrates,
all combining into a kilojoule of energy
to make possible
the long tight embrace of his wife
that he never wants to end.

He thought about saving up his morphine tablets
and taking them all at once
but fears his son would think him a coward.

He regrets shouting
and letting his anger get out of control.
He can't remember when their relationship deteriorated.
His son works in this Trust; was sure he saw him once looking at him in x-ray.
He knows it affects his wife, when he refuses to visit.
Feels responsible and wishes he'd been someone else.

Entering into conversations
at the bedside of patients
makes of you a clairvoyant.
There is a certain look,
silk thin skin, the loss of body mass,
these are the ones you won't be asking
the restaurant to order a taxi home.

V

The pharmacist listens for the screak of ice in difficult conversations

Come in, Laila. As-Salaam-Alaikum.
Like the game of hide and seek
you learnt early how to be discrete.
You always slip in here, quieter than air
seeking to hide in the shyness
but your hijab sings louder than the muezzin.

End of life drugs are always uncomfortable
to prescribe, sadness is expected.
Best to anticipate a difficult journey's end:
pain, sickness, secretions and agitation.

You remembered the drug boxes
stacked uneven on your mother's bedside table.
Made you wonder why she stopped smiling
and began sleeping for most of the time.

I was a bit nervous when he first saw me coming towards him.
I thought I saw his prejudice pull up a drawbridge.
Reluctantly, he surrendered,
coming down the stone stairs of his castle,
opening his wallet to show me his wife's photo.

When she died, you had to push hard
through your aunties to reach the bed,
too young to stay as long as you wanted to
but allowed to wear her apron in the kitchen.

The eldest of five sisters,
became their mother overnight:
a pillar to support your father,
preparing everyone's meals

often alone, doing the washing up
checking uniforms before school
attending parents' evenings.

Like the sun and air given without question
with an expectation to be always there
even after your father married again.

He wanted to know why so many drugs
and what they would do to him.
I stepped forward on thin ice
and felt I'd walked further out than with anyone else.
I wanted to walk backwards very slowly.

Then he asked: if I'd seen anyone die before
I felt the ice screak under my feet.
I nodded without words and he realised
I wasn't a foreigner to this country.

VI

The occupational therapist always finds solutions by climbing

Teresa, Teresa, when you rush in here
I feel there's so much energy in your urgency.
A patient wants to die at home and needs an assessment:
the peak of Mount Kilimanjaro appears through the clouds
and nothing's going to stop you from reaching it.

You drag discussions towards solutions
where other professionals see only problems.
Any house is adaptable:
move the settee against the wall,
put the dining table and chairs in the shed.

Just remember, she's losing everything.
She might need to hold on to something
and not lose her home to a huge
hospital bed filling up the front room.

I went through what was possible
and she apologised
saying she couldn't take any more in.
She wanted to tell me
how every time she sits beside him
she wants to tell him about the dog and the fridge talking
but he's struggling to keep his eyes open.
There are messages on the answering machine
asking if she's had an accident.

Sometimes, your father forgot
to collect you from school,
then the dialogue began
while walking home alone.

One day, he forgot he had any family
and the knife asked the arm:
'Did he leave because of me?'

He became an obstacle of a feeling
that you weren't good enough
but you decided to learn to climb.

Found healing in belaying others
up and over their own difficulties
and seeing the brightness of self-belief
upon reaching the top of what's impossible.

She knows he keeps worrying
about who is going to look after her
but she's always been the one who did the looking after.

They are unprepared for the emptiness
filling the room pretending to be silence

VII

The newly qualified nurse thinks some words can bite

Kirsty, Kirsty, you've usually gallons of energy.
Is this a different dress this morning?
On your insides: butterflies,
a churning stomach and a heart
pounding to get through your chest.

It's your amygdala translating
the 'what ifs' of thought
into sharp pokes of panic.
Feeling clammy, slight tremor?
Too much adrenaline

being pumped around your system.
Try Peter Pan's trick: think happy thoughts,
grab a big balloon of your happiest memory,
breathe deeply and let it carry you away within it.

When I enter the four bedded room
I thought it is best to avoid his eyes.
When I gave him his tablets, I thought he's going to ask me:
how long do I have left?
How would I know? I don't know what to say
and it freaks me out.

I usually fill in the silences;
I could jabber for England.
What if I say the wrong thing?
When his wife asks: is he getting any better?
I keep asking her to speak to the doctor.

I try to put myself in her position
but find myself nowhere; I've never had any one I know die before.
So, rather than look stupid, it's best to keep away from her.

You usually can't stop talking
but today you're quiet.
Last night a student nurse
doing whatever you were told;
today in a staff nurse's uniform
everyone expects you to have
the answers to all their questions.

For months you have walked through
these same doors and today it's not the same ward:
discharges, admissions, a constant challenge.
Drug rounds and observations can't be missed.
An arrest, a death, sucks any hope out of the air.
Social services are insisting we need a case conference
and a patient's getting angry because his pain is getting worse.

VIII

The junior doctor should test the depth before swimming with patients

Anna, Anna, when you first
came in here, it was difficult
to unravel why you chose medicine,
submerged under four years of theory.

Junior doctors must create a space
inside themselves big enough
to become a reservoir
continuously being filled to capacity.

Every patient's story flows in:
their ailments, history of illness,
their social background, until there isn't
much room for the you, you used to be.

Honesty and compassion help you swim
when the waters seem overwhelming.

My conversation got into a tangle.
I tried to swim with him towards the wall of the reservoir.
I encouraged him to step on the dry land of his own conclusion
but he became afraid, and fell into avoidance.

I watched the surface, but suspected he was diving deeper to hide from me.
In the end, I panicked and just came out with it:
'I think you are going to die
and we can't prevent it.'

Then his face emerged, changed.
I lifted myself out of the water
leaned forward and offered my hand.
He was tiring, trying to stay afloat.

I had thrown away any life jacket of hope
and now he wouldn't get in the boat.

IX

The consultant hears the rickety click of a stadium's turnstile

Christopher, every individual patient,
out of the pandemonium of their lives
tries to explain why they are feeling unwell.
You listen with such concern
that they think you are going to invite them home.

Someone asked about last week's patient.
You only need to make certain associations:
presenting problem, the circumstance,
maybe his background.
Then a row of neurons
illuminates the archives
and he appears from the darkness
in all his story, as if he was
drinking a cup of tea, sat in your kitchen.

In hindsight, I shouldn't have undertaken
the endoscopy this morning
but I let him persuade me.

It was the way he said it:
he enjoyed football but preferred cricket,
supported Middlesbrough but couldn't stand the Mackems.

'It is like this doc: when you're four nil down, ten minutes to go,
do you wave to be taken off
or fight until you can't carry on?'

He thought it was the ICI chemicals that did the business.
No Health and Safety protection back in them days.
Every corner of the plant had a different smell.

Even in the dark he knew where he was.
I suspect he'd digested so much pollution, it poisoned his biome.

I can take the weight, if I have to,
of twenty-eight people at any one time
and my metal spine starts to creak.
Every day, you carry the heavier expectations
of so many patients wanting to survive
but where do you put all that hope and disappointment?

You almost crawl down the camera
through the stomach and into the bowel.
The size and cluster of his polyps are enormous
and the bleed's coming from the varices.

You do realise before you retire
there will be over thirty thousand patients
occupying a space as large as Sunderland's
football stadium, somewhere inside you.

X

The ward sister imagines the Pietà beside the patient's bed

Rebecca, Rebecca, my lift always
feels lighter when you enter in here.
You see everyone as significant.
In your presence staff feel
better about themselves.
I've never heard a negative word said about you.

Other wards are always asking:
are there any vacancies coming up on twenty-four?
When the work's the busiest, you're out on the floor
making sure there's dignity in the care.
You set the standards and others
want to show how hard they can work for you.

The Chaplain heard someone crying behind
your office door, you kept saying you felt you'd failed.

No matter how many times I rerun the moment
it doesn't make me feel any better.
He'd just come back from Endoscopy
and the consultant said: just to keep him comfortable.
He vomited and his pyjama jacket needed changing.
His wife arrived; I asked her to give us ten minutes.

Come on, lift up your chin.
If you hadn't gone in
he could have been found alone
on the floor instead of in your arms.

I asked him, if he wouldn't mind putting his arms around me.
He raised his eyebrows, smiled and slowly rolled towards me.
Kirsty, the staff nurse, removed his jacket ever so carefully
then he unexpectedly vomited blood over me.

It just kept coming, on my hands and dress.
He became unconscious very quickly; I couldn't do anything to bring him back.
He had a DNACPR form, the notes said: approaching end of life.
I just held on to him, tried to clear his airway and then he died.

At times like this, I wish I had arms.
You eased the pain with your presence
and there's always gentleness in your voice.
He died holding on to someone.

While he was vomiting, his wife kept knocking
asking if she could come in yet.
She had a latte from Costa going cold.
I suspect she knew something was going on.

I couldn't have brought her into that, as a memory.
But who am I to decide? She could have been with him sooner.

XI

The cleaner keeps thinking about the Shroud of Turin and Rubik's Cube

Come on in, Dorothy.
I know the girls call you Dot.
Sometimes, I get the impression
that hospital cleaners learn how to be anonymous.

You quietly wipe germs into non-existence
with hands squeezed tight in bright latex blue.
You are ghosts roaming the corridors
purging surfaces of any infections.

Whenever you try to get under the beds
you always say the same thing: whoever
designed these overalls never had to work in them
and probably employs a house cleaner.

It's a shift of floors, stairs, my metal doors
and acknowledging how, in the end, we all become invisible.

It is strange not seeing him.
We used to talk about everything.

After the porters had taken him,
his bed was still warm.
It didn't seem right to clean it straight away.
His indentation was still on the mattress
reminded me of the Shroud of Turin.

He had a wicked sense of humour.
He took two sweeteners and no milk.
He hated having to have the catheter.
He asked me, if he wrote a letter to his son
would I make sure his wife got it?

I just kept looking around the bed
wondering if he was near and could he still hear me.

Dot, when you came for the job
no one said you'd see more
of men's private parts than
if you worked in a nudist colony.

You've seen every type of catheter,
nasal tube, chest drain and stoma
and discovered drawn curtains are useless
in keeping people's problems a secret.

He felt he could talk to you.
You'd quickly bring the nurse with pain relief.
You didn't need a thermometer and blood pressure
to tell you his condition was getting worse.

He felt his son was like a Rubik's Cube—
frustrating and too complicated to bring together.

XII

The porters push death along the corridors hoping no one notices

Even before the doors start to open
I know what's coming.
It is one of those brief few moments
when I think, maybe this is how I began.

Hospital porters stand
at either end of a long box
and suspiciously check my floor space
to see if I am empty before entering.

Heads always turn,
conversations cease,
and everyone knows this box
is an uncomfortable line across the ordinary.

The colourful drape, pretends it's not death
being pushed by, silently on wheels.

There is no place called here.
All around only the echo of words.
It's not what I thought, because I haven't got any of them, anymore.

I couldn't stop the vomiting,
desperately sorry for the ward sister.
I could see Doris, outside the door, with the latte, waiting.

I feel I must stay close to myself
while I am still warm.
Like not wanting to leave the bed in the morning.

There are no words here.
I am a song that has been sung,
a thought no longer remembered.

It is an utterly different way of being.
I can't explain; there isn't any effort, it's easier than living.

My metal container feels like a mortuary fridge:
fourteen hundred times a year,
twenty-five times a week, three times a day
and you are the first this morning.

The questions in here make me dizzy.
It's either a battle between eternity or nothingness.
Without a brain you can't probe for an answer.
'How can I experience anything of heaven?'

It can't be what we know because it is not a physical state.
I cannot know I'm dead. If I did, I wouldn't be
because I won't have consciousness
or maybe it's to do with parallel universes.

With memory left in the neurones of the brain
how will I know who I am anyway?

XIII

The son hopes God in his mercy remembers the belt

Ian, Ian, you've only just made it.
My sliding doors were reluctant.
They hesitated, but you squeezed in anyway.
Please don't have any big confrontation in here.

The porters would have stopped anyone
getting in, once the long box is occupied,
draped, and going down to the mortuary
but they knew who you were in your uniform.

You've surprised one of them when
you placed your hand firmly on the lid.
You're not letting him get away
without having the final word.

You've avoided this moment for years but
I can only give you four floors to say it all.

Ever since you were admitted,
I've said to myself; 'Go and reconcile with him.'
You don't know how many times I've been here
pacing up and down outside ward twenty-four.

Even now, I can still hear you and mam arguing,
muffled sounds coming up through the floorboards
and me under the covers, crying,
blocking up my ears from all the horrible things being said.

It always came to an end when Mam mentioned her name.
Then you'd hit her, then a long silent nothingness.
So many times, I thought you'd killed her.
So, when I'd come down the stairs to try and help her,

you'd be furious, roar and chase after me
swinging the belt with the buckle end.

Mam said it was complicated; you had a tough childhood, illegitimate,
abused in a care home. You know what? I couldn't give a fuck.

I was ten and you beat any kind of sympathy out of me.
You were strong, good at cricket, called me after Ian Botham.
You thought you'd make me tough.
You'd build in me backbone.
That's because you lacked one.

You were never kind.
I can see you now, standing over me, bulging eyes, red faced,
ranting, swinging it with all your righteousness.

Funny, never heard you having any fights with any men your own size.

You wanted forgiveness, a peaceful death, and a fitting end
but I keep hearing Mam crying. Now I'll tell you what I'll do: in your coffin
I'm going to wrap the belt around your hands instead of a rosary.

XIV

Feelings drained of emotions become mist and fog

Doris, it feels not all of you has entered in here;
there's a chill where you used to be.

Your emptiness turns
me into a vacuum.

Your thoughts are drifting
with no inclination to come together
or try and make any sense of things.

You watched the waxy shine
slowly cover him, until he looked still as stone.

Now you cannot leave the moment,
the room, the bedside.

This world has become an unfamiliar place.
You cannot fill or occupy any of it.
Today, everything seems to be swirls of mist and fog.

A plastic bag in either hand
full with the leftovers of a life.
Scales of unfairness weighing
only the DNA still attached
to the towel and pyjamas.

The whisper of warmth
from his wedding ring
on your finger
is all there's left of him.

A numbness deeper than my bone marrow,
asks: if there's any purpose in any of it.

Find him Lord, forgive him and bring him near.
The cleaner handed me a letter, and the ward sister was lovely.
I forgot to ask her if Ian had come when I wasn't there.

XV

The father's letter triggers a new narrative

Down here in the basement
where the heart of the hospital pulses,
your feet are stopping
my doors from closing.
Too drained to stand?
Three in the morning, lucky no one needs us.

You are a home on fire.
Even when calm, embers glow.
Your story will continue to consume you
if you keep fanning the flames.
Deny it oxygen, start a new sentence.

What is this incendiary past?
A scorched narrative where
the smoke of memory selectively remembers.

His words feel tender on the page.
Small squiggles, a regret of letters
lacking in confidence to rise and fall with any flair.
He wants to make it rain.
He's ashamed his anger ignited too quickly
and his snarl was petrol on any tenderness.

His legacy is ashes, his loss
never picking up the child in you.
Forgiveness has nothing to do with words.
It's understanding the importance of believing
in a different ending, where you find
a new door out of being the victim.

Lord, this steel floor is as cold
as he is tonight, alone, in the mortuary.

I grew when he watched me play football.
His joy when I scored or made a good tackle
that was the real him I never knew.

When we entered the games of make-believe
he was the child, liberated from his past
a door opened he could never find on his own.

Lord of all tangled stories
erase my resentment, growing like a cancer.
We never asked for this surprise of a life
and the randomness of who makes up our family
but my response to the challenges makes me who I am.

Lord, who lives across the border, bring him to a new adventure.
Let me see him happy in my dreams
and realize the self we have sculptured out of the time is all we get to keep.

Footnote

1 .Lourdes water is water which flows from a spring in the Grotto of Massabielle in the Sanctuary of Our Lady of Lourdes, France.

2. The Shroud of Turin, also known as the Holy Shroud, is a length of linen cloth bearing the negative image of a man. Some claim the image depicts Jesus of Nazareth.

A HOSPITAL CONVERSATION

Thoughts are incense
in the chilled breathing
of this evening air,
makes me more spirit than flesh.

I have walked
all around you,
through you,
worked on all your wards
up and down all of your stairs
and abseiled off your roof.

Sometimes I wonder
if you have entered into
the somewhere else in me.

Doors slide, open wide.
Staff, still occupied by patients,
look for their cars
feet fatigued from walking
seven miles of a shift.

Your ward lights on the top floor
are a reassurance, a beacon above the council houses,
keeping the darkness at a distance.

Your grey beams of cement
make broad reliable shoulders.
This image of you lives in me.
If I stare long enough
will I catch you...slightly moving?

Are we not in the womb of you?

Where do the words we say to each other go?
Where does the energy used disperse to?
What happens to the distance we've walked?
How much of us do your walls absorb?

If we could hear all the voices
all the words ever spoken in this place,
what would be its consistent chorus?

A pulse flickering in the ward light
up on the seventh floor
speaks in its own Morse code:

Every tap turned on is me.
The hum of the blood pressure cuff is me.
The squeak from the bed going down to X-ray is me.
The voice of the lift is me.
I am the rings in the telephone
and the squeal of the buzzers.
I speak though the oxygen and suction machine.
I even speak through the steam sputtering
from the coffee machine in the canteen

and every second of every minute I am saying:

Together we are the physicality of hope
restorers of dignity and peace
creators of space for goodness to grow.
We are the means and substance
by which all the best in us can surface.

SYNCHRONICITY

From a hospital side room
an emaciated woman beckoned me in.
She wore a bindi
said to cover concealed wisdom.

I didn't understand
what she meant by her whispered: Bhajan Bhajan.
I saw an Asian doctor in the corridor
and asked if she could help translate.

She wants you to pray over her.
She feels she is dying.

But I'm a Christian chaplain.
God's word is in the Bible.
I can get a Hindu priest.

She wants you. She likes your face. She wants you to pray over her.
I'll translate.

The traditional prayers became new
transformed from English into Hindi
with rhythms and sounds I'd never imagined before.

Within the last of the long-sung sentences
the woman left us.

Still, silent, we observed her absence.
The doctor was crying and said:

Thank you for inviting me
to be a part of such a privileged moment.
Never felt more human.
You probably didn't know
when you asked me but I'm a Muslim.

SHARP AS A NEEDLE

Anonymous, in a foetal position, concealed in a well-washed, oversized hospital nightdress, tousled hair, you watched my arrival through the bedside rail.

I fetched a spoon for your ice cream.
When I returned your easy smile opened up this clearing.

I commented on the strength in your muscly hand as we shook and you led me back into the factory where a younger self sits at a Singer,

feeling its rip-pithy rhythm, guiding moist thread through a steel needle's eye in a noisy thirty years of making John Colliers' fifty-shilling suits.

The doctor wondered about dementia when you replied 'train driver' to the question on occupation. A discourse on women's right to vote, the suffragettes, eased his concern.

Your hand helped me climb onto a miniature train, squeezed tight with children, you on the engine shouting 'All-a-board' around Albert Park most Saturday mornings.

The nurse interrupted with routine drugs, adjusted your naso-gastric tube and the ward routine shunted us back into the familiar.

THE MUSCLE IN THE HEART OF THE NHS.

You have come to the blue from all walks of life
with your faiths, customs and languages
making the NHS echo with accents.

The N is the necessity to give of your best
and gently comfort, at the end of life.
The H is for your hands, a stranger's touch,

taking blood, making patients feel they belong.
The S is for your skills, mature, experienced,
researched, focused on patients.

You have come to the blue where feet walk for miles
around beds, along corridors, giving out medicines,
looking for the vulnerable in each shift.

Covid twists loose emotions
and stretches to the limits
fibres until they tear.

Patients and their relatives see:
you treat people in the way you want to be treated
and in these waters, we are all trying to stay afloat.

You have come to the blue and today it asks:
leave your home and enter into the danger
of what you breathe, not knowing if you've become a carrier.

Be cautious and wear protection.
Be compassionate but remember you are not invincible.
Be open to discovering the nuances to being a human.

Your family need to hear the turn of your key in the door.
Bring home the heart of what you've been a part of.
In this service ask for grace from a God you do or don't believe in.

You are the blue in the swell of the storm,
powerless from the loss of what once felt secure,
tossed among huge waves.

Patients, sometimes couples, holding hands in isolation,
dying without any warning, after saying they were feeling better.
No preparation, within hours of each other. Texting 'Good Bye' to families.

Entering each room, all you can do is swim through
and back up to the surface. Uncover your own words. Be kind to each other.
Do what you can for the people you are trying to bring ashore.

AND THE DEAD WALKED THROUGH ME...

I remember the blue flashing through the curtains of the nursing home. I'd been unwell for days, couldn't catch my breath. I was made to wear a mask in the ambulance. The siren screaming made me think: must be serious.

I could see from the stretcher, along the corridor. A cleaner was bringing a brightness in straight lines to one side of the floor. I used to do that job. I saw doctors and nurses with lines on their cheeks, where the masks dug deep. They looked like they'd just been punched. I passed two porters talking. One said he'd pushed the long box to the mortuary more in one day, than he did in a week.

I saw my heart briefly running up and down the steep hills of a cardiac monitor. Then it was disconnected. I heard the words 'ceiling of care' spoken by a doctor through a mask.

I could see my son through the window, nervous, standing on his own. Looked like an extra from Star Wars. *One nurse said when working long shifts she needed the bladder of a whale; made me laugh. The TikTok on the nurse's iPhone lightened the atmosphere, turning everyone into a dancing queen.*

I'd been on this ward many times before but this time the buzzers were strangely quiet. The ward clerk, in gloves, mask and visor, kept wiping everything twice. I overheard the doctors saying they were becoming experts in hospice care. One nurse said if her breath came through the mask, making a cloud on the plastic, she'd probably catch it.

I felt better; then something changed, felt even worse. I was exhausted; there was nothing to cling on to. I'd entered somewhere the oxygen couldn't reach me.

THE WOLF AT THE DOOR

She hears scratching,
convinced she's locked it,
bolted it, nailed a plank across it.

Constantly listening
for the sound of breathing
on the other side.

On the ward, a growing intolerance
to machine-forced oxygen: frightened patients
unable to complete their sentences.

Families on FaceTime
gather around phones
trying to keep their loved-ones from being taken.

Individuals who have never known illness
members of the same household
torn apart without warning.

She keeps checking,
eyes fixed on the handle,
blaming herself for failing to protect.

Words are a poor camouflage.
She can't see there are no walls
only a doorframe and door

and a wolf that prowls between breaths.

THE AUTOPSY OF A DEATH

The metronome of my heart
keeps the music of me alive.

When it slows
my blood is an ooze of lava.

From my skin
the colour retreats from the surface.

When oxygen cannot nourish
the hemispheres, my brain becomes a desert.

The night sky of consciousness
dims until all the lights go out.

Whoever I have become
is gone in a whisper.

I cannot know. I am
without any awareness.

I cannot feel anything
without my spinal cord.

I cannot remember
without any neurotransmitters.

I am not in a place.
I am an absence, an emptied space.

If I am anywhere, I am in the pause
after the last word of any poem.

READ POEMS AS PRAYERS

—A phrase taken from Heaney's Station Island *(1984)*

We always hoped someone else was looking for us.
In this house, where words were rough as gravel
no one cared what we heard:
the aggressive thump of sentences:
a screeched phrase *it's all your fault*
often ending in the smashed dishes of shame.

Books on shelves in other people's houses
made our empty walls more acoustic.
We never learned to listen
to alternative perspectives
or feel the stillness, when the reasonable
brings in a hush to arguments.

Parents abused innocent sentences,
forced them to become accomplices.
They loved to shove a knife of a phrase
in deep to find the only hiding place,
mocking any defence with the way it was said.
We provoked all their assonance in words like bastards.

Now, without warning, whenever I hear compassion spoken,
its arm feels gentle around my shoulders.
Its squeeze is for me,
asking me to follow to somewhere deep
deeper than before I was born
to a place where all I can do is wail   without end.

Down here words are tense, apprehensive;
they dream of being light as Gregorian chant.
They are convinced I kiss like Judas.
If they could, they'd spit me out.
They don't trust me. I make them nervous.
I infect their beauty because I am all the fuck of fury!

But they are the needle in my compass.
Only they can bring me home
to a place waiting in the lost and found
where laughter dances to the unexpected,
where hands outstretched only want to catch,
where I am all lullabied.

When the hum and smile of the rhythm and the half rhyme
lead to where feelings no longer have to hide—
there, the line trembles:
I am home in a new turn of phrase.
There, words redeem
and all the past is prayer.

A NOTE ON THE AUTHOR

Mel McEvoy was born in Liverpool in 1959 to Irish Immigrants who were grateful to live on a council estate. He spent a period of time in the Catholic religious life and has lived in North East England since 1982. A nurse for thirty-nine years in the NHS, for the last twenty years he has been a Nurse Consultant in Palliative and End of Life Care. Mel received a Master of Arts in Creative Writing with Distinction from the Open University in December 2019.

ACKNOWLEDGEMENTS

'Living in an Empty House' was published in *As Above So Below*—online poetry magazine. P25 Issue 3 Summer 2019.

Three poems in *These Are the Hands*—NHS Anthology, March 2020, Fair Acre Press. 'Living in an Empty House'; 'Do Your Own Dead Come for You'; 'He Swims in the Silence'.

'The Shape and Size of My Sister's Coffin' was published in *Secret Chords: A Poetry Anthology of the Best of the Folklore Prize* (2021). Folklore Publishing Limited.

'And the Dead Walked Through Me' was published in *NARRATIVES OF COVID: Loss, Dying, Death and Grief During COVID-19* (2021). Collection of short essays /poems, Open University.

A NOTE ON THE TYPE

This book of poems is set in Requiem, the American type designer Jonathan Hoefler's 1992 typeface based on inscriptional capitals found in Ludovico Vicentino degli Arrighi's 1523 writing manual, *Il Modo de Temperare le Penne.* Requiem is a distinguished contemporary typeface with a beautiful italic and well suited to a text in which a predominant note is that of elegy.